THE JOKES EVERY 11 YEAR OLD SHOULD KNOW

FUNNY KIDS JOKES
TO MAKE YOU LAUGH

HOLLI WHALING

∽ DEDICATION ∽

To all the 11-year-olds
who know that
laughter is the best superpower.
Keep sharing your jokes,
spreading smiles,
and owning your awesome
sense of humor.
This book is for you—keep
being legendary! 😎😂

TABLE OF CONTENTS

INTRODUCTION

Welcome to the Ultimate Joke Book
for 11-Year-Olds! 😎

Hey there, comedy champs!

If you're ready to level up your laugh game, you've come to the right place. This book is packed with jokes that are guaranteed to make you chuckle, snicker, and maybe even roll your eyes (in the best way possible, of course). Whether you're the class clown, the quiet genius with the best one-liners, or just someone who loves a good laugh, we've got something here for you.

Get ready to crack up your friends, leave your family in stitches, and maybe even impress your teachers with your epic sense of humor. So, flip the page, dive in, and get ready to become the ultimate joke master!

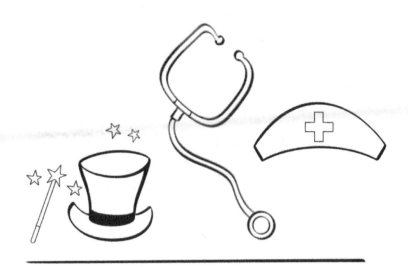

CHAPTER 1:
OCCUPATIONS JOKES

This chapter has the 13 best
Occupation jokes

WHAT DO YOU CALL BABIES IN THE ARMY?

Infantry

WHY DID THE BIOLOGIST BREAK UP WITH THE PHYSICIST?

They had no chemistry

DID YOU HEAR HOW THE PERSONAL TRAINER QUIT THEIR JOB?

They gave their too weak notice

WHAT KIND OF JOB CAN YOU GET AT A BICYCLE FACTORY?

Spokesperson

DID YOU HEAR ABOUT THE RANCHER WHO HAD 97 COWS IN HIS FIELD?

When he rounded them up,
he had 100!

DID YOU HEAR ABOUT THE GUY WHO INVENTED THE KNOCK-KNOCK JOKE?

He won the "no-bell" prize!

WHY DID THE NURSE HAVE A RED CRAYON?

To draw blood

HOW DO SUBWAY CONDUCTORS KNOW WHERE TO GO?

Training

IF A BUTCHER WEARS A SIZE XL SHIRT AND A SIZE 13 SHOE, WHAT DOES HE WEIGH?

Meat.

HOW DO LUMBERJACKS KNOW HOW MANY TREES THEY'VE CUT DOWN?

They keep a log

WHAT DID THE METEOROLOGIST SAY WHEN THEY TRIED TO CATCH FOG IN THEIR HANDS?

"I mist."

WHAT DO YOU CALL A MAGICIAN WHO'S LOST HIS MAGIC?

Ian

WHY DID THE SCARECROW WIN AN AWARD?

Because he was outstanding in his field!

WHEN HE ACCEPTED HIS AWARD WHAT DID HE SAY FOR HIS ACCEPTANCE SPEECH?

Hay, it's in my jeans!

Chapter 2:
Food Jokes

This chapter has the 16 best
Food jokes

WHY WAS THE COOKIE SO SAD?

Because his mom was
a wafer so long

WHICH VEGETABLE DO SAILORS HATE THE MOST?

Leeks

WHAT DO YOU GET WHEN YOU COMBINE A CHRISTMAS TREE WITH A COMPUTER?

Pine-Apple

WHAT DO YOU CALL CHEWBACCA WITH COOKIES IN HIS BEARD?

A chocolate chip Wookie

HOW DOES DARTH VADER LIKE HIS TOAST?

On the dark side!

WHAT'S A NOODLE'S FAVORITE ACTION MOVIE?

Mission impastable

WHAT IS A SCARECROW'S FAVORITE FRUIT?

A Strawberry

WHAT WAS THE MATH TEACHER'S FAVORITE DESSERT?

Pi

WHY DID THE JELLYBEAN GO TO SCHOOL?

To become a Smartie

WHAT WAS THE TORTILLA CHIP'S FAVORITE HOBBY?

Salsa Dancing

WHAT DID THE GRAPE SAY WHEN HE WAS PINCHED?

Nothing, he gave a little wine.

WHICH FRIENDS SHOULD YOU TAKE TO LUNCH?

Your taste buds

WHAT DOES A CONDIMENT WIZARD PERFORM?

Saucery

HOW DID THE BURGER KING PROPOSE TO HIS GIRLFRIEND?

With an onion ring.

WHAT DID THE CHEESE SAY
TO THE OTHER CHEESE
ON ITS BIRTHDAY?

You feta have a gouda birthday

WHAT DID THE LETTUCE
SAY TO THE CELERY?

Quit stalking me

CHAPTER 3:
MATH JOKES

This chapter has the 11 best
Math jokes

WHY IS
THE OBTUSE TRIANGLE
ALWAYS SO FRUSTRATED?

Because it's never right

WHY DO PLANTS HATE MATH?

Because it's full of square roots!

WHAT DO YOU CALL TWO GUYS WHO LOVE MATH?

Algebros!

WHY SHOULD YOU NEVER TRUST SOMEONE WRITING ON GRAPH PAPER?

Because they must be plotting something!

WHAT DID THE 90° ANGLE SAY AFTER AN ARGUMENT?

"It turns out, I was right!"

WHY COULDN'T THE ANGLE GET A LOAN?

Because his parents wouldn't cosine!

HOW DO YOU STAY WARM IN ANY ROOM?

Go to the corner—it's always 90 degrees.

WHAT DO YOU CALL A NUMBER THAT CAN'T STAY IN ONE PLACE?

A roamin' numeral!

DID YOU HEAR ABOUT THE MATHEMATICIAN WHO'S AFRAID OF NEGATIVE NUMBERS?

He'll stop at nothing to avoid them!

WHO INVENTED FRACTIONS?

Henry the 1/4th!

DID YOU KNOW THAT 10 + 10 AND 11 + 11 ARE THE SAME?

It's true!

10 + 10 = 20 and 11 + 11 equals twenty too!

Chapter 4:
HISTORY Jokes

This chapter has the 7 best
History jokes

WHY IS THERE NO KNOCK-KNOCK JOKE ABOUT AMERICA?

Because freedom rings

WHAT DID KING GEORGE THINK OF THE AMERICAN COLONISTS?

He thought they were revolting.

WHAT DID THE FLAG DO WHEN IT LOST ITS VOICE?

It just waved.

WHAT DID THE COLONISTS WEAR TO THE BOSTON TEA PARTY?

Tea-shirts

WHERE WAS THE DECLARATION OF INDEPENDENCE SIGNED?

On the bottom of the page.

WHY IS HISTORY LIKE A FRUIT CAKE?

It's full of dates.

HOW DID LOUIS XIV FEEL AFTER COMPLETING THE PALACE OF VERSAILLES?

Baroque

WHERE WAS THE DECLARATION OF INDEPENDENCE SIGNED?

at the bottom

CHAPTER 5:
AROUND THE WORLD Jokes

This chapter has the 4 best
Around the world jokes

WHAT DO YOU CALL A FRENCH MAN IN SANDALS?

Phillipe Phloppe

WHAT WORLD CAPITAL HAS THE FASTEST GROWING POPULATION?

Ireland.
The capital is Dublin every day

WHAT'S THE BEST THING ABOUT SWITZERLAND?

I don't know, but
the flag is a big plus!

HOW WAS THE ROMAN EMPIRE CUT IN HALF?

With a pair of Caesars

CHAPTER 6:
SCHOOL JOKES

This chapter has the 11 best
School jokes

HOW MUCH DO NEUTRONS COST?

Nothing, they're free of charge

WHAT'S THE EASIEST WAY TO GET STRAIGHT A'S?

Use a ruler

WHAT DID THE STUDENT SAY WHEN THE TEACHER ASKED WHY HE MISSED THE FIRST DAY OF SCHOOL?

Actually Ma'am I didn't miss it at all

WHAT CANDY DO YOU EAT ON THE PLAYGROUND?

Recess pieces

THE THERMOMETER SAYS WHAT TO THE GRADUATED CYLINDER.

You have graduated, but I have more degrees than you.

WHY DID THE READER GIVE UP ON PRIDE AND PREJUDICE?

The characters were too Austentatious.

WHERE DO MATH TEACHERS GO ON VACATION?

Times Square

WHAT WAS SOCRATES' FAVORITE THING TO MOLD?

Play dough (Plato).

WHAT DID THE ENGLISH TEACHER LIKE TO EAT FOR BREAKFAST?

Synonym rolls

WHY DID SHAKESPEARE ONLY WRITE IN PEN?

He couldn't decide which type of pencil to use—a 2B or not 2B

WHAT DID ONE DNA STRAND SAY TO THE OTHER?

Does my bum look big
in these genes?

WHAT IS THE BLACKBOARD'S FAVORITE DRINK?

Hot Chalk-o-late

CHAPTER 7:
ANIMALS JOKES

This chapter has the 12 best
Animals jokes

WHAT DO YOU CALL AN ANT WHO FIGHTS CRIME?

A vigilante!

WHAT DO YOU CALL AN EXPLODING MONKEY?

A Bab-boom.

WHAT DO YOU CALL
AN ELEPHANT THAT DOESN'T
MATTER?

Irrelephant

WHAT DO DOGS AND PHONES
HAVE IN COMMON

Collar ID

WHAT IS IT CALLED WHEN A CAT WINS A DOG SHOW?

A cat-has-trophy

WHAT KIND OF JOBS DO FUNNY CHICKENS HAVE?

They are comedi-hens!

WHAT KIND OF CAT LIKES LIVING IN WATER?

An octo-puss.

WHAT'S THE DIFFERENCE BETWEEN A CAT AND A SENTENCE?

One has claws at the end of its paws, the other has a pause at the end of its clause.

HOW TO BEARS KEEP COOL?

They use bear-conditioning.

WHAT'S
THE BEST WAY TO WATCH
A FISHING TOURNAMENT?

Live stream

HOW DOES A PENGUIN BUILD ITS HOUSE?

Igloos it together

WHAT DO YOU CALL AN ILLEGALLY PARKED FROG?

Toad

CHAPTER 8:
SPORT JOKES

This chapter has the 16 best
Sport jokes

WHERE DO SPORTS TEAMS GO TO BUY NEW UNIFORMS?

New Jersey

WHAT'S A GOLFER'S FAVORITE LETTER?

Tee!

WHAT IS HARDER TO CATCH THE FASTER YOU RUN?

Your breath!

HOW DO HOCKEY PLAYERS PREFER TO BE PAID?

With a check.

WHY IS TENNIS SUCH A LOUD SPORT?

The players raise a racquet.

WHERE DO THEY KEEP THE LARGEST DIAMOND IN NEW YORK CITY?

Yankee Stadium

WHAT IS A CHEERLEADER'S FAVORITE FOOD?

Cheerios!

WHY DON'T YOU EVER DATE A TENNIS PLAYER?

Because love means nothing to them

WHY DID
THE BALLERINA QUIT?

Because it was tu-tu hard!

WHAT DO MESSI AND
A MAGICIAN HAVE
IN COMMON?

Both have plenty of
HAT-TRICKS

WHAT DID
THE BASEBALL GLOVE SAY
TO THE BALL?

Catch ya later!

HOW DO BASEBALL PLAYERS
STAY CONNECTED?

They touch base every
now and then.

WHY DID
THE FOOTBALL COACH YELL
AT THE VENDING MACHINE?

They wanted
their quarter back!

A PITCHER RAISES
ONLY ONE LEG WHEN
THROWING A BALL, WHY?

If they raise both the legs,
they will fall down.

WHAT DO SPRINTERS EAT BEFORE A RACE?

Nothing. They fast!

WHY DID THE SQUARE AND TRIANGLE GO TO THE GYM?

To stay in shape.

CHAPTER 9:
VIDEO GAME JOKES

This chapter has the 16 best
Video game jokes

WHY IS FRENCH MARIO SO GOOD AT PREDICTING THE FUTURE?

He uses his L'ouija board

WHY CAN'T PC GAMERS USE UBER?

Too many incompatible drivers.

WHAT DO AMERICANS DO AFTER WINNING THE WORLD CUP?

Turn off the PlayStation.

WHAT DO YOU GET WHEN YOU CROSS SONIC THE HEDGEHOG AND CURIOUS GEORGE?

2 Fast 2 Curious

WHY DOESN'T MARIO LIKE TO USE THE INTERNET?

He's afraid of the Browsers.

WHAT DID MARIO SAY WHEN HE BROKE UP WITH PRINCESS PEACH?

"It's not you; it's a me, Mario!"

IT WOULD BE SO NICE
IF SONIC ADDED AN E
TO THE END OF HIS NAME

Get it?? Sonice

WHAT DOES A GAMER USE
TO MAKE BREAD?

Ninten-dough.

HOW DO MINECRAFT PLAYERS CELEBRATE?

They throw block parties

WHAT GAME DO YOU PLAY AFTER EATING TACO BELL?

Fartnite

I ASKED A NINTENDO FAN TO HELP ME CHANGE A LIGHT BULB.

He wasn't very helpful, he just kept playing with the switch.

WHAT DO YOU SAY WHEN YOU LOSE A NINTENDO GAME?

I want a wii-match!

YESTERDAY I GOT AN XBOX FOR MY LITTLE BROTHER.

Best trade ever!

WHAT DID THE LEPRECHAUN SAY WHEN THE VIDEO GAME ENDED?

Game clover!

WHAT KIND OF SWIMWEAR DOES SONIC THE HEDGEHOG WEAR WHEN HE GOES TO THE BEACH?

Speedos

WHY DID THE XBOX ONE EAT ITS CEREAL FOR BREAKFAST, BUT NOT ITS PANCAKES?

It had the spoon,
but not the 4k.

I RECENTLY BROKE UP
WITH MY
VIDEO GAME CONSOLE...NOW
IT'S MY EX-BOX.

It was nothing personal,
it was just time for a Switch.

CHAPTER 10:
MISCELLANEOUS JOKES

This chapter has the 32 best
Miscellaneous jokes

WHEN IS A DOOR NOT A DOOR?

When it's ajar

WHAT HAPPENED WHEN BLUEBEARD FELL OVERBOARD IN THE RED SEA?

He got marooned!

WHY DID THE IPHONE WALK INTO THE WATER?

He was wading for a phone call

WHY COULDN'T THE SKELETON GO TO SCHOOL?

His heart just wasn't in it.

WHY DO TEENAGERS TRAVEL IN GROUPS OF THREES AND FIVES?

Because they can't even!

WHAT DO YOU CALL IT WHEN HAGRID TAKES A CERAMICS CLASS?

Hairy Potter

WHY DID IT TAKE SO LONG FOR A MAN TO EAT A CLOCK?

It was very time-consuming.

WHAT DID ONE TECTONIC PLATE SAY TO ANOTHER WHEN THEY BUMPED INTO EACH OTHER?

Sorry, my fault

HOW DO YOU DROWN A HIPSTER?

In the mainstream.

WHY DO RAPPERS NEED UMBRELLAS?

Fo' drizzle.

WHY DO COUPLES WHO GO TO THE GYM TOGETHER NEVER BREAK UP?

They always work it out

DID YOU HEAR ABOUT THE TWO GUYS WHO STOLE A CALENDAR?

They each got six months.

WHY DO PIMPLES MAKE THE WORST KINDS OF PRISONERS?

Because they keep breaking out all the time!

WHY DON'T YOU MAKE FRIENDS WITH VAMPIRES?

Because they're pains in the neck

WHAT IS ORANGE AND RED AND FULL OF DISAPPOINTMENT?

High school pizza

WHAT DID JAY-Z CALL HIS GIRLFRIEND BEFORE THEY GOT MARRIED?

Feyoncé

WHAT'S THE DIFFERENCE BETWEEN A WELL DRESSED MAN ON A UNICYCLE, AND A POORLY DRESSED MAN ON A BICYCLE?

Attire

WHAT KIND OF TEA IS HARD TO SWALLOW?

Reali-tea

WHAT DID THE FAMILY SAY WHEN THEY LOST 25% OF THEIR ROOF?

Oof

WHY DID THE FIRECRACKER GO TO THE HAIR SALON?

It needed to trim its bangs.

WAITER! WAITER! THIS COFFEE TASTES LIKE SOIL.

Yes, sir, it was ground this morning.

WHY DID THE OPERA SINGER GO ON A CRUISE?

She wanted to hit the high Cs.

WHAT DO YOU CALL A SNOWMAN WITH A SIX-PACK?

An abdominal snowman

WHAT DO YOU GET WHEN YOU CROSS CAPTAIN AMERICA WITH THE INCREDIBLE HULK?

The star-spangled Banner.

HOW DID THE YETI FEEL WHEN HE HAD FLU?

Abominable

WHICH IS THE BEST DAY TO GO TO THE BEACH?

Sunday

WHAT PART OF A CAR NEEDS THE MOST SLEEP?

The muffler, it's always exhausted

WHAT DO YOU GET WHEN YOU DIVIDE A JACK O' LANTERN BY ITS DIAMETER?

Pumpkin Pi

WHAT HAPPENS WHEN YOU WEAR A SNOW SUIT INSIDE?

It melts all over the carpet.

HOW DID THE HIPSTER BURN HIS MOUTH?

He had pizza before
it was cool

WHY SHOULD'T YOU TRUST TREES?

They seem kinda shady

WHAT'S THE DIFFERENCE BETWEEN IGNORANCE AND APATHY?

Don't know, don't care.

CHAPTER 11:
RIDDLES

This chapter has the 14 best Riddles

KATE'S MOTHER HAS THREE CHILDREN: SNAP, CRACKLE AND ___?

Kate! It's Kate's mother, after all.

I GO UP AND DOWN, BUT NEVER MOVE. WHAT AM I?

A staircase

WHAT IS THAT ONE THING THAT YOU CAN NEVER THROW BUT ALWAYS CATCH?

It's your breath.

WHO SHAVES MULTIPLE TIMES A DAY AND STILL HAS A BEARD?

The barber

WHAT HAS THIRTEEN HEARTS, BUT NO OTHER ORGANS?

A deck of cards

YOU'RE RUNNING A RACE AND AT THE VERY END, YOU PASS THE PERSON IN 2ND PLACE. WHAT PLACE DID YOU FINISH THE RACE IN?

You finished in 2nd place

SHARKS BELONG TO WHICH PLACE?

Finland

WHICH WORD BECOMES SHORTER WHEN YOU ADD 2 LETTERS TO IT?

The word "short."

THERE ARE 3 APPLES IN THE BASKET AND YOU TAKE AWAY 2. HOW MANY APPLES DO YOU HAVE NOW?

You have 2 apples. You took away 2 apples and left 1 in the basket.

WHAT HAS FOUR LEGS BUT CAN'T WALK?

A table

I AM AN ODD NUMBER.
TAKE AWAY A LETTER AND
I BECOME EVEN.
WHAT NUMBER AM I?

Seven

ZOEY HAS A VERY BIG FAMILY.
SHE HAS 20 AUNTS, 20 UNCLES
AND 50 COUSINS. EACH OF HER
COUSINS HAS AN AUNT WHO IS
NOT ZOEY'S AUNT. HOW IS THIS
POSSIBLE?

Their aunt is Zoey's mom!

TWO FATHERS AND 2 SONS
SPENT THE DAY FISHING,
BUT ONLY CAUGHT 3 FISH.
THIS WAS ENOUGH FOR EACH
OF THEM TO HAVE ONE FISH.
HOW IS THIS POSSIBLE?

There were only 3 people fishing. There was one father, his son, and his son's son. This means there were 2 fathers and 2 sons, since one of them is a father and a son.

MRS. BROWN HAS 5 DAUGHTERS. EACH OF THESE DAUGHTERS HAS A BROTHER. HOW MANY CHILDREN DOES MRS. BROWN HAVE?

They have 6 children. Each daughter has the same brother. There are 5 daughters and 1 son

CHAPTER 12:
ONE LINERS

This chapter has the 12 best
One liners jokes

I try to tell chemistry jokes but....
there's no reaction.

A police recruit was asked during
the exam,
"What would you do if you had to
arrest your own mother?"
He said,
"Call for backup."

I'm reading a book about anti-gravity...It's impossible to put down!

The past, present and future walked into a bar.
It was tense.

Sometimes I tuck my knees into
my chest and lean forward.
That's just how I roll.

I thought I'd tell you a brilliant
time-travel joke,
but you didn't like it.

Two silk worms had a race. It
ended in a tie.

Light travels faster than sound;
we all know that.
What can it mean?
That most people look bright
before you hear them speak.

Someone stole my mood ring. I'm not sure how I feel about that.

I love pressing F5. It's so refreshing.

If you clean a vacuum cleaner,
you then become a
vacuum cleaner.

Two wrongs don't make a right.
But two Wrights did make an
airplane!

We hope you enjoyed reading this book as much as we enjoyed creating it! Please consider leaving us a review where you purchased the book. If you have any jokes you'd like to share, we'd love to highlight them in our next book! Please send them to Bestjokesforkids@gmail.com. Scan the QR below to see the other books in our series.

Made in the USA
Las Vegas, NV
19 November 2024

12154490R10066